THE JPS B'NAI MITZVAH TORAH COMMENTARY

Va-yeshev (Genesis 37:1–40:23)
Haftarah (Amos 2:6–3:8)

Rabbi Jeffrey K. Salkin

The Jewish Publication Society · Philadelphia
University of Nebraska Press · Lincoln

INTRODUCTION

News flash: the most important thing about becoming bar or bat mitzvah isn't the party. Nor is it the presents. Nor even being able to celebrate with your family and friends—as wonderful as those things are. Nor is it even standing before the congregation and reading the prayers of the liturgy—as important as that is.

No, the most important thing about becoming bar or bat mitzvah is sharing Torah with the congregation. And why is that? Because of all Jewish skills, that is the most important one.

Here is what is true about rites of passage: you can tell what a culture values by the tasks it asks its young people to perform on their way to maturity. In American culture, you become responsible for driving, responsible for voting, and yes, responsible for drinking responsibly.

In some cultures, the rite of passage toward maturity includes some kind of trial, or a test of strength. Sometimes, it is a kind of "outward bound" camping adventure. Among the Maasai tribe in Africa, it is traditional for a young person to hunt and kill a lion. In some Hispanic cultures, fifteen year-old girls celebrate the *quinceañera*, which marks their entrance into maturity.

What is Judaism's way of marking maturity? It combines both of these rites of passage: *responsibility* and *test*. You show that you are on your way to becoming a *responsible* Jewish adult through a public *test* of strength and knowledge—reading or chanting Torah, and then teaching it to the congregation.

This is the most important Jewish ritual mitzvah (commandment), and that is how you demonstrate that you are, truly, bar or bat mitzvah—old enough to be responsible for the mitzvot.

What Is Torah?

So, what exactly is the Torah? You probably know this already, but let's review.

The Torah (teaching) consists of "the five books of Moses," sometimes also called the *chumash* (from the Hebrew word *chameish*, which means "five"), or, sometimes, the Greek word Pentateuch (which means "the five teachings").

Here are the five books of the Torah, with their common names and their Hebrew names.

> ➤ **Genesis (The beginning), which in Hebrew is Bere'shit (from the first words—"When God began to create").** Bere'shit spans the years from Creation to Joseph's death in Egypt. Many of the Bible's best stories are in Genesis: the creation story itself; Adam and Eve in the Garden of Eden; Cain and Abel; Noah and the Flood; and the tales of the Patriarchs and Matriarchs, Abraham, Isaac, Jacob, Sarah, Rebekah, Rachel, and Leah. It also includes one of the greatest pieces of world literature, the story of Joseph, which is actually the oldest complete novel in history, comprising more than one-quarter of all Genesis.
>
> ➤ **Exodus (Getting out), which in Hebrew is Shemot (These are the names).** Exodus begins with the story of the Israelite slavery in Egypt. It then moves to the rise of Moses as a leader, and the Israelites' liberation from slavery. After the Israelites leave Egypt, they experience the miracle of the parting of the Sea of Reeds (or "Red Sea"); the giving of the Ten Commandments at Mount Sinai; the idolatry of the Golden Calf; and the design and construction of the Tabernacle and of the ark for the original tablets of the law, which our ancestors carried with them in the desert. Exodus also includes various ethical and civil laws, such as "You shall not wrong a stranger or oppress him, for you were strangers in the land of Egypt" (22:20).
>
> ➤ **Leviticus (about the Levites), or, in Hebrew, Va-yikra' (And God called).** It goes into great detail about the kinds of sacrifices that the ancient Israelites brought as offerings; the laws of ritual purity; the animals that were permitted and forbidden for eating (the beginnings of the tradition of kashrut, the Jewish dietary laws); the diagnosis of various skin diseases; the ethical laws of holiness; the ritual calendar of the Jewish year; and various agricultural laws concerning the treatment of the Land of Israel. Leviticus is basically the manual of ancient Judaism.

> Numbers (because the book begins with the census of the Israelites), or, in Hebrew, Be-midbar (In the wilderness). The book describes the forty years of wandering in the wilderness and the various rebellions against Moses. The constant theme: "Egypt wasn't so bad. Maybe we should go back." The greatest rebellion against Moses was the negative reports of the spies about the Land of Israel, which discouraged the Israelites from wanting to move forward into the land. For that reason, the "wilderness generation" must die off before a new generation can come into maturity and finish the journey.

> Deuteronomy (The repetition of the laws of the Torah), or, in Hebrew, Devarim (The words). The final book of the Torah is, essentially, Moses's farewell address to the Israelites as they prepare to enter the Land of Israel. Here we find various laws that had been previously taught, though sometimes with different wording. Much of Deuteronomy contains laws that will be important to the Israelites as they enter the Land of Israel—laws concerning the establishment of a monarchy and the ethics of warfare. Perhaps the most famous passage from Deuteronomy contains the *Shema,* the declaration of God's unity and uniqueness, and the *Ve-ahavta,* which follows it. Deuteronomy ends with the death of Moses on Mount Nebo as he looks across the Jordan Valley into the land that he will not enter.

Jews read the Torah in sequence—starting with Bere'shit right after Simchat Torah in the autumn, and then finishing Devarim on the following Simchat Torah. Each Torah portion is called a parashah (division; sometimes called a *sidrah,* a place in the order of the Torah reading). The stories go around in a full circle, reminding us that we can always gain more insights and more wisdom from the Torah. This means that if you don't "get" the meaning this year, don't worry—it will come around again.

And What Else? The Haftarah

We read or chant the Torah from the Torah scroll—the most sacred thing that a Jewish community has in its possession. The Torah is written without vowels, and the ability to read it and chant it is part of the challenge and the test.

But there is more to the synagogue reading. Every Torah reading has an accompanying haftarah reading. Haftarah means "conclusion," because there was once a time when the service actually ended with that reading. Some scholars believe that the reading of the haftarah originated at a time when non-Jewish authorities outlawed the reading of the Torah, and the Jews read the haftarah sections instead. In fact, in some synagogues, young people who become bar or bat mitzvah read very little Torah and instead read the entire haftarah portion.

The haftarah portion comes from the Nevi'im, the prophetic books, which are the second part of the Jewish Bible. It is either read or chanted from a Hebrew Bible, or maybe from a booklet or a photocopy.

The ancient sages chose the haftarah passages because their themes reminded them of the words or stories in the Torah text. Sometimes, they chose *haftarah* with special themes in honor of a festival or an upcoming festival.

Not all books in the prophetic section of the Hebrew Bible consist of prophecy. Several are historical. For example:

The book of Joshua tells the story of the conquest and settlement of Israel.

The book of Judges speaks of the period of early tribal rulers who would rise to power, usually for the purpose of uniting the tribes in war against their enemies. Some of these leaders are famous: Deborah, the great prophetess and military leader, and Samson, the biblical strong man.

The books of Samuel start with Samuel, the last judge, and then move to the creation of the Israelite monarchy under Saul and David (approximately 1000 BCE).

The books of Kings tell of the death of King David, the rise of King Solomon, and how the Israelite kingdom split into the Northern Kingdom of Israel and the Southern Kingdom of Judah (approximately 900 BCE).

And then there are the books of the prophets, those spokesmen for God whose words fired the Jewish conscience. Their names are immortal: Isaiah, Jeremiah, Ezekiel, Amos, Hosea, among others.

Someone once said: "There is no evidence of a biblical prophet ever being invited back a second time for dinner." Why? Because the prophets were tough. They had no patience for injustice, apathy, or hypocrisy. No one escaped their criticisms. Here's what they taught:

> God commands the Jews to behave decently toward one another. In fact, God cares more about basic ethics and decency than about ritual behavior.
> God chose the Jews *not* for special privileges, but for special duties to humanity.
> As bad as the Jews sometimes were, there was always the possibility that they would improve their behavior.
> As bad as things might be now, it will not always be that way. Someday, there will be universal justice and peace. Human history is moving forward toward an ultimate conclusion that some call the Messianic Age: a time of universal peace and prosperity for the Jewish people and for all the people of the world.

Your Mission—To Teach Torah to the Congregation

On the day when you become bar or bat mitzvah, you will be reading, or chanting, Torah—in Hebrew. You will be reading, or chanting, the haftarah—in Hebrew. That is the major skill that publicly marks the becoming of bar or bat mitzvah. But, perhaps even more important than that, you need to be able to teach something about the Torah portion, and perhaps the haftarah as well.

And that is where this book comes in. It will be a very valuable resource for you, and your family, in the b'nai mitzvah process.

Here is what you will find in it:

> A brief **summary** of every Torah portion. This is a basic overview of the portion; and, while it might not refer to everything in the Torah portion, it will explain its most important aspects.
> A list of the **major ideas** in the Torah portion. The purpose: to make the Torah portion real, in ways that we can relate to. Every Torah portion contains unique ideas, and when you put all

of those ideas together, you actually come up with a list of Judaism's most important ideas.

> Two ***divrei Torah*** ("words of Torah," or "sermonettes") for each portion. These *divrei Torah* explain significant aspects of the Torah portion in accessible, reader-friendly language. Each *devar Torah* contains references to **traditional** Jewish sources (those that were written before the modern era), as well as **modern** sources and quotes. We have searched, far and wide, to find sources that are unusual, interesting, and not just the "same old stuff" that many people already know about the Torah portion. Why did we include these minisermons in the volume? Not because we want you to simply copy those sermons and pass them off as your own (that would be cheating), though you are free to quote from them. We included them so that you can see what is possible— how you can try to make meaning for yourself out of the words of Torah.

> **Connections:** This is perhaps the most valuable part. It's a list of questions that you can ask yourself, or that others might help you think about—any of which can lead to the creation of your *devar Torah.*

Note: you don't have to like everything that's in a particular Torah portion. Some aren't that loveable. Some are hard to understand; some are about religious practices that people today might find confusing, and even offensive; some contain ideas that we might find totally outmoded.

But this doesn't have to get in the way. After all, most kids spend a lot of time thinking about stories that contain ideas that modern people would find totally bizarre. Any good medieval fantasy story falls into that category.

And we also believe that, if you spend just a little bit of time with those texts, you can begin to understand what the author was trying to say.

This volume goes one step further. Sometimes, the haftarah comes off as a second thought, and no one really thinks about it. We have tried to solve that problem by including a **summary** of each haftarah, and then a mini-sermon on the haftarah. This will help you learn how these sacred words are relevant to today's world, and even to your own life.

All Bible quotations come from the NJPS translation, which is found in the many different editions of the JPS TANAKH; in the Conservative movement's *Etz Hayim: Torah and Commentary;* in the Reform movement's *Torah: A Modern Commentary;* and in other Bible commentaries and study guides.

How Do I Write a *Devar Torah?*

It really is easier than it looks.

There are many ways of thinking about the *devar Torah.* It is, of course, a short sermon on the meaning of the Torah (and, perhaps, the haftarah) portion. It might even be helpful to think of the *devar Torah* as a "book report" on the portion itself.

The most important thing you can know about this sacred task is: *Learn* the words. *Love* the words. Teach people what it could mean to *live* the words.

Here's a basic outline for a *devar Torah:*

"My Torah portion is (name of portion)_____,
    from the book of _____, chapter

_____.

"In my Torah portion, we learn that_____
    (Summary of portion)

"For me, the most important lesson of this Torah portion is (what is the best thing in the portion? Take the portion as a whole; your *devar Torah* does not have to be only, or specifically, on the verses that you are reading).

"As I learned my Torah portion, I found myself wondering:

> ➤ *Raise a question that the Torah portion itself raises.*
> ➤ *"Pick a fight"* with the portion. Argue with it.
> ➤ *Answer a question* that is listed in the "Connections" section of each Torah portion.
> ➤ *Suggest a question to your rabbi* that you would want the rabbi to answer in his or her own *devar Torah* or sermon.

"I have lived the values of the Torah by _____
(here, you can talk about how the Torah portion relates to your
own life. If you have done a mitzvah project, you can talk about
that here).

How To Keep It from Being Boring
(and You from Being Bored)

Some people just don't like giving traditional speeches. From our per-
spective, that's really okay. Perhaps you can teach Torah in a different
way—one that makes sense to you.

> ﹥ Write an "open letter" to one of the characters in your Torah por-
> tion. "Dear Abraham: I hope that your trip to Canaan was not too
> hard . . ." "Dear Moses: Were you afraid when you got the Ten
> Commandments on Mount Sinai? I sure would have been . . ."
> ﹥ Write a news story about what happens. Imagine yourself to
> be a television or news reporter. "Residents of neighboring cit-
> ies were horrified yesterday as the wicked cities of Sodom and
> Gomorrah were burned to the ground. Some say that God was
> responsible . . ."
> ﹥ Write an imaginary interview with a character in your Torah portion.
> ﹥ Tell the story from the point of view of another character, or a mi-
> nor character, in the story. For instance, tell the story of the Gar-
> den of Eden from the point of view of the serpent. Or the story
> of the Binding of Isaac from the point of view of the ram, which
> was substituted for Isaac as a sacrifice. Or perhaps the story of
> the sale of Joseph from the point of view of his coat, which was
> stripped off him and dipped in a goat's blood.
> ﹥ Write a poem about your Torah portion.
> ﹥ Write a song about your Torah portion.
> ﹥ Write a play about your Torah portion, and have some friends act
> it out with you.
> ﹥ Create a piece of artwork about your Torah portion.

The bottom line is: Make this a joyful experience. Yes—it could
even be fun.

The Very Last Thing You Need to Know at This Point

The Torah scroll is written without vowels. Why? Don't *sofrim* (Torah scribes) know the vowels?

Of course they do.

So, why do they leave the vowels out?

One reason is that the Torah came into existence at a time when sages were still arguing about the proper vowels, and the proper pronunciation.

But here is another reason: The Torah text, as we have it today, and as it sits in the scroll, is actually *an unfinished work*. Think of it: the words are just sitting there. Because they have no vowels, it is as if they have no voice.

When we read the Torah publicly, we give voice to the ancient words. And when we find meaning in those ancient words, and we talk about those meanings, those words jump to life. They enter our lives. They make our world deeper and better.

Mazal tov to you, and your family. This is your journey toward Jewish maturity. Love it.

THE TORAH

❖ Va-yeshev: Genesis 37:1–40:23

Welcome to the longest story in Genesis, and one of the most famous in the entire Bible—the story of Joseph. Joseph is Jacob's favorite child, although he is a bit of a jerk to his brothers. Joseph is constantly bragging to his brothers about his dreams of grandeur, and this really annoys them. Eventually they plot to do away with Joseph, throw him into a pit, and then sell him to some traders who are on their way to Egypt.

Joseph winds up as a slave in Egypt, working for the captain of Pharaoh's guard. He is doing pretty well (for a slave) until a false accusation lands him, once again, into the "pit" of a prison cell. Yes, life is the "pits" for Joseph—until you realize that a pit (like a peach pit) can be the seed of new growth. Joseph will grow up. Stay tuned.

Summary

> Jacob's favorite child is his second-youngest son, Joseph. Jacob makes him a special coat, which stirs up jealousy in his brothers. Joseph also has dreams of grandeur, which does not win him any popularity contests with his brothers, either. (37:1–11)

> Joseph's brothers get fed up with his bragging, and they sell him to some Midianite traders, who take him to Egypt. And, there, Joseph is sold to Potiphar, the captain of Pharaoh's guard. (37:12–36)

> A side story about Judah shows how he wrongs his daughter-in-law, Tamar. Judah has relations with her, and later Judah must publicly admit his wrongdoing. (38:1–30)

> In the first case of sexual harassment in the Torah, Potiphar's wife hits on the handsome Joseph. When he resists, he winds up in prison. (39:1–23)

> The always-talented Joseph interprets the dreams of his fellow prisoners, but they forget what he did for them. (40:1–23)

The Big Ideas

› **Parents should treat their children equally.** Parents should not play favorites. Jacob made it clear to everyone that he loved Joseph best, and this created terrible jealousy within his family.

› **Even seemingly "small" actions can have massive consequences.** Jacob spoiled Joseph. While this might have appeared to be a small matter at the time, it had terrible results. It ultimately resulted in the entire Jewish people becoming enslaved in Egypt. The small stuff counts.

› **Dreams are important.** Our dreams tell us a lot about what is going on inside our heads, and so we ought to pay attention to them. Often, they represent things that we are worried about. In the Bible they can sometimes even predict the future.

› **Being honest with yourself is the mark of maturity.** In particular, the best leaders are those who can own up to their mistakes, apologize, and then move on to do better. Judah's admission that he was wrong is an example of this. Perhaps that is why his tribe became the most important tribe, and why Jews, to this day, bear his name—Judah-ites, which means "Jews."

› **Temptation is an ever-present reality.** Temptation always exists, whether it involves cheating, irresponsible sex, stealing or misusing money, or abusing power. It takes great strength and maturity to stand up to those temptations.

› **Jews have a role to play in their societies.** Here, Joseph is the historical role model for Jewish engagement in the world, because he devotes his efforts to improving the Egyptian economy. Jews have always brought their talents and their gifts to the countries and societies in which they live.

Divrei Torah

DON'T PLAY FAVORITES!

Here's a story that's all too common: Mother dies—she had been old, and she had lived a good life. One of her sons has always loved the antique dining-room table that used to be the setting for their warm family dinners. That's the only thing of his parents that he wanted. Instead, his mother made it clear before her death that his younger sister would get the dining-room table. He wound up with a simple bookcase. Yes, it is nice—but it is not the same as the antique dining-room table. That table had all the good memories built into it. But, now, it will never sit in his home. It will sit in his sister's house. He is jealous of his sister, and the anger burns inside him.

Sound familiar? It should. It's the story of Joseph, updated for our time. Joseph's brothers may have been jealous about his "amazing technicolor dreamcoat," but what they really wanted was their father's attention and affection.

Why did Jacob favor Joseph? He was born when Jacob was already quite old. Perhaps the mere existence of Joseph reminded him that he was still young enough to produce children! Or, perhaps Joseph looked like Jacob's beloved wife, Rachel, who dies when giving birth to her second son, Benjamin. Jacob had fallen instantly in love with Rachel; every time he saw Joseph, he relived that moment of falling in love.

Parental favoritism is the Genesis family pattern. Remember Sarah favoring Isaac, Rebekah favoring Jacob, and Isaac favoring Esau? It is what we would nowadays call "dysfunctional."

There are two lessons here.

First, when parents play favorites, it breeds deep resentment and anger that can go on for generations.

And the second—our actions can have unintended consequences. "A parent should never single out one child among the others, for on account of a piece of silk, which Jacob gave Joseph in excess of his other sons, his brothers became jealous of him and the matter resulted in our descent into Egypt." Joseph's brothers' jealousy over that one silk coat was the tipping point of the resentment that eventually led not just to their brother's slavery, but that of the entire Jewish people in Egypt.

But wait. Maybe God needed Joseph to be taken to Egypt, so that the Jewish people would wind up in Egypt, and eventually experience the Exodus from Egypt. As Bible scholar Avivah Zornberg writes: "[Joseph's brothers] find themselves in the chaos of a reality whose plot is hidden from them." Could it be that there is a greater reason for what happens to Joseph and his family that they themselves cannot discern?

Maybe this is all part of God's Big Plan. And maybe our actions are as well.

JUDAH AND TAMAR: THE EPISODE THAT CREATED THE JEWISH FUTURE

How did the Jews get their name?

Simple. The word "Jew" comes from the Southern Kingdom of Judah (the Northern Kingdom was Israel)—and, before that, from the tribe of Judah, which got its name from Jacob's son Judah. In Hebrew, the name Judah is Yehudah, which means "thanks" (from the same root as *todah*), because Leah was thankful to God after the birth of her fourth child (Judah).

But what was so special about Judah that the Southern Kingdom of ancient Israel and later the Jewish people were named after him, and that King David and his dynasty should be descended from him?

After the brothers sell Joseph into slavery, Judah wanders off from his troubled family, and marries, and has three sons. He marries the first son to a woman named Tamar; the son dies. He marries the second son to Tamar; he dies as well. There is still a third son waiting in the wings. Judah tells his daughter-in-law to wait around for that third son to grow up so that they can marry.

Why is that important? According to the biblical law known as levirate marriage, if a man dies, a surviving male relative must marry the widow so that they can have children. With two brothers dead and one left, the surviving son should have married Tamar so that they could have children. But Judah didn't give that son to Tamar. Therefore as the only other man in the family, Judah would have had to marry his daughter-in-law so they could have children and continue the family line. But, he doesn't. (And, don't worry: this tradition no longer exists).

Tamar knows that Judah has done wrong by not giving her his third son, or by not marrying her himself. He "owes" her children. And, so, she disguises herself as a prostitute, and she has sex with Judah—in order to get pregnant. Judah doesn't have enough "cash" on hand to pay her, so he leaves some of his belongings behind as a pledge that he will return and pay her later. Tamar, the "prostitute," becomes pregnant. Meanwhile, Judah finds out that his former daughter-in-law, Tamar, is pregnant—and she is unmarried! Big scandal! And here's the big deal—Judah doesn't realize that he has had sex with his own daughter-in-law, and he surely doesn't know that he has impregnated her!

Look at how Tamar handles the situation. She sends Judah's belongings to him, with the message that the man who left those things with her had impregnated her. As Rabbi Geela-Rayzel Raphael teaches: "Tamar refuses to publicly humiliate Judah. She does not report directly that Judah is the father; rather, she sets it up so that he confesses." Judah realizes that he has, by mistake, had sex with his daughter-in-law. He realizes that he should have married Tamar all along. He declares: "She is more in the right than I am!" (38:26). The ancient sages taught: "Why did Judah's descendants deserve to become kings? Because he admitted that he had done wrong."

Yes, when it comes to biblical stories about sex, this story is a little "out there." But Judah's sin is not the most important thing here; it is the way that he owns up to it. Ever since Cain denied moral responsibility for his brother, Abel, God has been waiting for someone to own up, publicly, to doing wrong. Judah is the first person in the Torah to do that. He will do so a second time when he steps forward to Joseph. Our tradition says that's why the Jews are named for Judah—because he could say, "I'm sorry."

Connections

> Joseph not only bragged to his brothers about his dreams; he also brought bad reports about them to his father. In other words, he was a tattletale. What is this story teaching us about gossip? Have you ever experienced gossip? What was it like?

> Do you know of siblings who are jealous of each other? What are some things in a family that can provoke jealousy? How do you think that parents should deal with this?

> Have you ever been in a situation where you had to own up to something you had done wrong? How did it feel? What did you learn from that? Can you think of historical examples of people who publicly confessed that they were wrong? Why is this trait particularly important in a leader?

> Have you ever faced a particular temptation (taking money, cheating on a test, doing anything that is wrong)? How did you deal with that temptation? Were you successful in resisting it? What does it take to fight temptations?

> Tamar refuses to accuse Judah in public. She does not want to humiliate him. Why is public humiliation so bad? How can it be avoided?

> Have you ever done something for a friend and felt that he or she was not particularly grateful to you? Did you ever feel "forgotten" by that friend? What was that experience like? How did

THE HAFTARAH

❖ Va-yeshev: Amos 2:6–3:8

"It's not just about us." That's what you can imagine the prophet Amos saying. He was a native of Tekoa, a village south of Jerusalem in Judah, but he moved to the Northern Kingdom of Israel. In the passage before the beginning of this haftarah, Amos went on a whirlwind tour of the other nations in the ancient Middle East, criticizing their human rights violations. The kingdoms of Israel and Judah must have thought that they were going to get off easy. No such luck. He scolded them too.

According to Amos the violations of Judah and Israel came about because they had broken the covenant with God. The biggest evidence? They had mistreated the poor. How had they done this? They took garments as collateral for loans. They drank wine that had been purchased with money from fines that they imposed on others. Amos is furious: look at how the people are acting, and compare that to how God had treated them during their wandering in the wilderness. Finally, Amos reminds the Jewish people of the meaning of being a Chosen People—not that they are special, but that God will hold them accountable for their sins.

What's the connection to the Torah portion, which describes how Joseph's brothers sold him into slavery in Egypt? In the haftarah, Amos quotes the Lord saying, "Because they have sold for silver those whose cause is just, and the needy for a pair of sandals" (2:6). Both are about "selling out" for the wrong reason. The brothers turned on one of their own and sold their very own sibling. The people of Amos's time turned on the most vulnerable in their midst. It's been said that when Joseph's brothers sold him, the amount of money they received was enough for each of them to buy a pair of sandals. How sad, especially when history repeats itself.

Chosen—For What?

An English journalist, William Norman Ewer, once wrote this little verse:

How odd
Of God
To choose
The Jews.

To which someone replied:

Not so odd
The Jews chose God.

Welcome to one of the most basic but controversial ideas in Judaism. It's the Chosen People, and it has a starring role in this haftarah.

How basic is it? So basic that Jews affirm it whenever we make *Kiddush* over wine, or say the blessing over the Torah. We say: "who has chosen us from all the peoples. But what does it mean? The verse in the blessing continues "and given us the Torah." The idea is that God chose the Jews to bring Torah into the world. In the words of writer Blu Greenberg: "We are chosen to serve as a witness to the world: how to live as an ethical community, a responsible and kind family, a caring neighbor, a believing spirit."

Being chosen in this sense is a mission; it doesn't mean privilege or that we are better than other people. To the contrary, the prophet Amos (see last week's haftarah) put it this way: "You alone have I singled out of all the families of the earth—that is why I will call you to account for all your iniquities" (3:2). Amos goes on say how God cares for other people too, but that Israel bears a special burden.

Throughout history some people have loathed the Jews for their notion of being chosen, some have admired it, and some have envied it.

Among Jews themselves some have denied it or felt embarrassed by it, while many have embraced it. Mordecai Kaplan and the Jewish Reconstructionist movement dropped the reference to the Chosen People altogether on theological grounds. And other Jews have found it too difficult to bear the burden of being chosen for historical reasons. To be chosen means, sometimes, to be persecuted. As Tevye famously jokes in *Fiddler on the Roof*: "God, I know that we're Your Chosen People. But could you choose another people for a change?"

Yet many if not most Jews find the belief in their chosenness to be a source of comfort and strength. Author Dennis Prager puts it rather starkly: "If I did not believe that the Jews were chosen by God, I would not raise my children as Jews. To bequeath the suffering that may attend being Jewish to my descendants is defensible only if we have a divine calling."

Some Jews prefer to call themselves "the choosing people" rather than "the Chosen People." Either way, it's a big responsibility—and the choice is ours!

❖ Notes

CPSIA information can be obtained
at www.ICGtesting.com
Printed in the USA
LVHW08s0951050818
585984LV00004B/440/P

9 780827 613676